FINALLY...

THE 24 HOURS OF LE MANS ENDURANCE RACE

Sam W. McQuade

CHAPTER TITLES

Le Mans, France, Sunday, June 19, 2016.........1

Why Le Mans?...5

My Porsche Experience……………………………..17

Porsche Driving Schools……………………………..33

24 Hours of Le Mans Facts………………………….57

The 24 Hours of Le Mans…………………………...61

Some Technical Stuff……………………………….…73

Experiencing the 24 Hours of Le Mans……….77

End of the 2016 Running of the 24 Hours of Le Mans………………………………………………….91

Le Mans, France, Circuit de la Sarthe, Sunday, June 19, 2016, 2:57 PM

Three minutes to go in the 84th running of the 24 Hours of Le Mans endurance race; Toyota #5 has a 1:40 second lead over Porsche #2, having passed it late morning. I am standing on my seat in the second row in the main grandstand above the pits from which I can see the start/finish line.

The crowd is looking left to Virage Ford, straining to see the Toyota emerge onto the grandstand straightaway for the final lap and victory, Toyota's first with its LMP1 Hybrid in five attempts. But, to everyone's shock, instead of accelerating it glides to a silent stop on the right side of the track, just past the start/finish line.

I hear in English: "What's the matter with the Toyota?"

Someone replies, "Must be waiting for the other Toyota to catch up so they can cross the finish line together."

But I think to myself: "Impossible; that car is in third place, four laps down."

One minute, forty seconds isn't very long at Le Mans racing speeds. Porsche #2, accelerating out of Virage Ford, screams across the finish line to a waving checkered flag, followed by the other 43 cars still on the course (44 of 60 cars that started manage to finish the race).

As silently as it stopped the #5 Toyota glides out onto the track to make a final lap, but it takes more than six minutes to complete the circuit and is disqualified.

The Porsche fans are screaming in giddy excitement. The big screen across from my seat shows the Japanese man who is the head of the Toyota LMP1 Racing Team with his head in his hands in obvious anguish and frustration. I think: "The only thing more appropriate would be watching him commit seppuku (Japanese ritual suicide)."

Later in our group's hospitality area, sponsored by Greaves Motorsports, an English team that had an entry in the LMP2 category, I asked Mr. Greaves what he thought had happened to Toyota #5.

"It ran out of gas."

Which, if true, would have been ironic, as the day before we got to visit the Greaves pit during the race; a question was asked about the bank of computer monitors, manned by several of the pit crew. The Greaves' Pit Boss was our host, and he explained that every function of the car is constantly monitored during the race: tire wear, temperature, oil pressure, etc., but *most importantly* fuel consumption. He said, "The dumbest thing any team can do at Le Mans is run the car out of gas while it is on the track."

With a one minute, forty second lead the Toyota could have made a quick refueling stop without losing the lead.

I asked Greaves, "Then how did the car manage to start back up and make a final lap?"

"The driver had to sit while the other cars finished for the batteries to charge; then it came in on hybrid electric power."

Which explains why it made no sound.

But the only people at the time who really knew what had happened to Toyota #5 was the

Toyota Team. Not the spectators in the stands. Nor Greaves.

Turns out that sometime prior to its abandoning the race, something happened to the turbo-intercooler connection, shutting down the combustion engine. Porsche #2 was rapidly closing the gap.

The 24 Hours of Le Mans is an endurance race, the toughest, most demanding and dangerous race in the world. Leading it during the race might get you kudos. The only thing that counts is finishing.

Preferably, in first place.

Why Le Mans?

Honestly, I don't know.

As a kid growing up in the 50s and 60s I knew every car make, model, and the year of manufacture. I had a veritable catalog in my head, because each year there were always styling changes, some radical, to hold car buyer interest in "the latest thing." It was also a form of planned obsolescence.

My Dad's opinion was that a car with 60,000 miles should be traded in for a new one. He had a good reason: cars in that time, with their old push-rod engines, usually didn't last much beyond 60,000 miles. He also wanted the latest body style and any new gizmos Detroit had invented.

My interest in cars had nothing to do with the cars Dad drove: only Buicks, mostly station wagons. About as exciting as owning a Dodge Caravan today. "Family Cars." Although he did buy Mom a used 1959 Cadillac Sedan de Ville, a yacht of a car, decked out with a ton of chrome and tailfins sporting four big red bullet shaped tail lights: the car in which I drove my date to prom my senior year.

I loved '60s muscle cars. What kid didn't?

My first car was a '65 Olds 442 with a Hurst four-on-the-floor transmission. "442" stood for: four barrel carburetor, four speed manual transmission, and twin tail pipes. Like the Beach Boys' "Little Deuce Coupe," I could get rubber in all four gears. I bought it used in June, 1966, after my freshman year at St. John's University in central Minnesota, a Catholic, male-only college connected to a Benedictine monastery. We freshmen had to obtain written permission from our dormitory floor prefect to leave campus. My floor prefect was a Benedictine monk, who, each time we asked for a pass, would say, "Why would you boys want to leave my version of Utopia?"

Girls, for one.

The girls in the city of St. Cloud. Not the girls in the sister College of St. Benedict, in a small town some five miles from the SJU campus, who were a collection of homely wallflowers.

When I returned to my home in Bismarck, ND, after that freshman year, I told Dad I wasn't going back to St. John's without a set of wheels, because to leave campus we had to hitchhike, which I told him felt dangerous. He agreed; hence the 442 purchase. What I didn't tell Dad was that only upperclassmen were allowed to have cars on campus.

That September, after unloading my stuff in the dorm room, my roommate and a couple of classmates and I drove into St. Cloud to the Bratwurst Haus for pitchers of 3.2 beer and brats. They were ecstatic; I would be driving them to SJU AWAY football games and to the Twin Cities on weekends.

They asked me, "How are you going to get a parking permit since you are only a sophomore?"

I said, "No idea."

Registration day I got my class schedule, and walked to the table with a sign: "Parking Permits." The senior manning the table was a dead ringer for Greggie, the nerd president of the snob fraternity in the movie, "Animal House," the guy whose fate after college was to get buggered in prison as a convicted aide to President Nixon. He asked me what I wanted, and when I told him I needed a parking permit, he pushed a paper form at me to fill out.

I had to bend over to write on the table. He was seated, so my head was at the level of his, when he said, "Hey, wait just a doggone minute here! You can't have a parking permit!"

I looked across at him.

"Why not?"

"Cuz you're just a sophomore."

It was one of my coming-of-age moments.

"Too late, asshole! My car is sitting in the east parking lot, and that is where it is going to stay, or I'm leaving this hole you call a college!"

Apparently Greggie had never been so addressed.

"Well, ok, then."

And that is how I became the first sophomore in the history of St. John's University to have a legal car on campus.

Having my 442 on campus meant freedom. Except when it wouldn't start during Minnesota cold snaps; the engine simply refused to start if the temperature fell below zero degrees (F). Attempts at jump-starting the battery from another car, or even being pushed halfway around Stearns County by a wrecker truck were futile.

But I had dreams of greater freedom.

It wasn't my idea to attend St. John's University. It was Mom's.

When I was a junior in high school she asked me where I was thinking of attending college. I said, "Tulane University." Without even knowing where Tulane University is located. I liked reading William Faulkner, which was pretty good for a high school kid, and I had developed a fascination for the Deep South; for some reason I associated Faulkner with Tulane.

This was long before Google. I don't know how Mom found out that Tulane is located in the city of New Orleans.

"No son of mine is going to a college in the den of iniquity of America! You are going to St. John's to get a nice Catholic education."

She was overlooking the fact that I had received my share of "nice Catholic education" in grade school and high school.

So, once enrolled in SJU, I knew I was stuck, no matter how much I wanted to go somewhere else. But, by chance, one day after beginning fall semester classes, I saw a notice on the dining hall bulletin board; several seniors had returned from a year at L'Universite de Sorbonne in Paris, and they were having an informal discussion about their experience.

Well, it all sounded pretty exotic: their descriptions of travels throughout France and Europe, the adventures they had lived and the sites they had visited.

There was just one problem: they had not passed the year-end written exam, so they had not been passed on to the oral exam, both requisites in France to be allowed to go onto the next level of studies.

Also they couldn't speak French.

But they still wanted a full year's credit for having "studied abroad."

This wasn't the first time SJU administration had faced this problem. So, in steps Miss Pettis, the newly appointed Chairperson of the French Department and Director of Studies Abroad.

Miss Pettis was new to St. John's, but she wasn't new; she was in her '70s, a life-long bachelorette (read: "man hater") in an all-male institution. To say she was the new – and first – Chairperson of the French Department was not saying much; formerly it had consisted of two monks who could barely speak French. But she went at it with a passion. As to being the new – and first – Director of Studies Abroad, she attacked that with a vengeance; she was "Christ come to cleanse the Temple."

I declared my intention to study in Europe my junior year by making an appointment for an interview with Father Dunstan, who was Dean of Academic Affairs. He was an affable sort, told me "Good Luck!" and, with a wink, passed me on to Miss Pettis.

In my first encounter with her, she

seemed to take an instant disliking to me. I don't know why. I was very polite to her. She handed me a questionnaire she had created regarding study abroad, told me to fill it out and return it to her office; after perusing it she would interview me in person.

I remember the questionnaire was quite lengthy, but I only remember the first "question," which really wasn't a question:

"State two reasons why you want to study in Europe your junior year."

That was easy.

I wrote:

1) Buy a Porsche 912 at the factory in Stuttgart;
2) Attend the 24 Hours of Le Mans.

I have no idea whence either of these ideas originated. At the time I owned one of the ultimate American muscle cars. So why a Porsche? And Le Mans? I was an avid listener on the radio of the Indianapolis 500, but I had never been to a car race, not even dirt track stock car races in Bismarck. And I knew nothing about NASCAR, which, in those days was considered Southern "Bubba," and not televised.

All I knew was that I wanted to buy a Porsche 912 at the factory in Stuttgart, and attend the 24 Hours of Le Mans, while studying my junior year in Europe, thousands of miles away from what we students called the "Pine Curtin" that was St. John's University.

I submitted my completed questionnaire to Miss Pettis's secretary, who informed me that I would be contacted for a follow-up interview.

Which didn't start well.

Miss Pettis began by telling me in no uncertain terms that the two responses I had written to justify her approval for my studying abroad were ridiculous, and that she was rejecting my application.

It was another of my coming-of-age moments.

I told her, politely and diplomatically, that I had a 3 point something grade point average, that I had provided her the requisite letters of recommendation by former and current teachers, and that my parents could afford my year in Europe.

I could tell by her reaction she was stuck.

She asked me what study abroad programs interested me, and I replied, "The University of Loyola in Rome." Because the classes were in English, and the brochure stated, "Class loads are purposefully light in order to allow students to travel and explore Italy and other European countries."

Miss Pettis, who had been around the study abroad block more than once, was having none of it; she described the Loyola of Rome program as a "year-long European lark!"

The only way she would approve my application was if I agreed to study in France, since I was already in my second year of French at SJU, and she didn't want me to waste it.

I said, "Well, the 24 Hours of Le Mans race is in France, right."

She said, "Of course it is."

She seemed most pleased.

She pulled some forms from her desk drawer, which I could see were already filled in.

"The Institute of European Studies, based in Chicago, has two centers in France: Paris and Nantes. I have taken the liberty to enroll you in the '67-68 summer and academic year courses in Nantes."

I said, "I have never heard of Nantes, France. Why not Paris?"

"Because I don't want you distracted by all the distractions."

Ol' Miss Pettis had set me up.

I left Bismarck for France in June of 1967. I returned in July, 1968, with a beautiful French fiancée, a 3.9 grade point average in French studies, fluent in French, and a Porsche 912 I bought at the factory in Stuttgart for $4,125. After ten months and 20,000 miles I sold it to a guy in Minneapolis for $4,125 to marry my French fiancée; good investment, as we have now been married 47 years.

But until this year, 2016, age 69, I had never been to the 24 Hours of Le Mans.

MY PORSCHE EXPERIENCE

Like, "Why Le Mans?" "Why Porsche?"

Although I am a Porsche guy now, honestly, I don't know.

My '65 Olds 442 muscle car, metallic green, was long, wide, with 350 plus horsepower; I could burn the rear tires in all four gears. It was great for "dragging Main" in Bismarck; the only guys who could beat me drove "Goats:" Pontiac GTOs. The 442 was sleek for its time, with only trim and bumpers in understated chrome.

My sophomore year, between homework in my dorm room, I drooled over the Porsche catalog of 1968 models: 912, 911T, 911L, and 911S.

I wanted to buy a 911S, the top-of-the line model, with a six cylinder, horizontally opposed engine, over 200 horsepower. But it cost $6,000 plus at the factory.

Working on the trucks two summers for our family beer distributorship, I had saved around $3,000. A 912 was $4,125 at the factory: four cylinder, horizontally opposed, 115 HP engine, designed by the founder, Ferdinand Porsche, who had designed the Tiger tank for Hitler. Dad said he would pay the difference.

$4,125 in 1967 was a lot of money for a car. But Dad was paying more than $3,000 for his Buicks. So the difference then is not the price disparity that exists today between Porsches and comparable performance cars.

Although I had placed my order for a beige color Porsche 912 in early June, 1967, before I left home for France, because of some dealership screw-ups, it wasn't ready for a factory delivery until just before the Christmas holidays.

Dan, a Nantes classmate, and I boarded the train for Stuttgart, Germany, at Gare de l"Est in Paris, the station from which trains departed Paris for points east. We rented a cheap hotel room in Stuttgart and set out to find a place for dinner, finding only crowded, noisy, and smoky beer halls. We picked one; the menu was in German, which neither of us knew. Nobody in the hall spoke English, much less French. A buxom Teutonic-looking waitress said something guttural to us that we deciphered as, "You are now in Germany **UND** you must speak

German!" The only words I knew in German other than, "Seig, Heil!" which I thought might not go over too well, were "bratvurst und bier," which we were served along with the usual dollops of potatoes and sauerkraut.

I have this theory of why Germans waged war against their neighbor countries for so many years: the only things they eat come in animal casings. While guarding their borders, wearing those heavy steel spiked helmets, they would sniff: "What are they cooking over there?"

The next morning we got checked in at the reception desk of the Porsche factory, and a guy who spoke English gave us a tour. It was fascinating to see, because, although there was an assembly line of sorts, everything, from moving Porsche bodies hanging from hooks in ceiling tracks to assembling engines was done by hand.

Most of the employees were drinking beer from what looked like Mason jars. In the painting room a half-dozen men wearing big mitts were rubbing the shine into the last coat of paint on a 911 or 912 body; occasionally they paused to remove a mitt and guzzle beer from their Mason jar.

I asked our guide, "What in the hell is going on here?"

"The factory is about to close two weeks for Christmas holidays. We're just letting the boys get a jump start."

I said, "Oh, yeah? When was my car built?"

"Don't worry; before the beer drinking started."

At the end of the tour we were escorted to a waiting area. After some minutes a young man who appeared to be in his late twenties, dressed in a business suit, entered and asked, "Which one of you is Sam McQuade?" When I got up from my chair he stared at me with Germanic coldness for a long, uncomfortable moment.

"How old are you?"

"Twenty. I will be twenty-one in April."

"Do you have *ANY* idea how many Germans much older than you can afford a Porsche?"

I said, "Sir, I do not."

Shaking, he screamed, "**NOBODY!**"

The only thing missing from his tirade was the Nazi stiff arm salute.

I wanted to remind him which country had lost two world wars.

But I didn't.

I mumbled something about having worked for my father in our family beer business and that I had saved up most of the purchase price.

Which didn't seem to satisfy him in the least.

To him I was obviously just a spoiled American brat.

Dan and I followed him as he goose stepped us to a drive-through garage. Several awkward minutes of silence ensued before a garage door opened on one end and my Porsche was driven in. The driver hit the accelerator just a bit before shutting down the engine, which responded with that unmistakable Porsche growl.

Herr Kraut informed me the car had been thoroughly test-driven; the only thing I needed to do was not rev the engine more than 5,000 rpm, 6,000 being the "red line," the first 1,000 kilometers.

Dan and I both couldn't wait to get away from the guy before one or the other of us started WWIII. We tossed our bags in the front trunk, jumped in, and were off to Austria to join up with a group of Parisian kids for a Christmas skiing vacation.

I was cruising about 90 MPH, when Dan yelled I was about to miss the turn south toward Austria. I braked hard, downshifting from fifth gear to second while revving the engine, the tachometer topping 5,000 rpm, then dropping to under 1,000, as I made the turn.

A deafening explosion erupted from the rear-mounted engine, scaring hell out of us, and making my stomach collapse.

I slumped forward, my forehead on the top of the steering wheel.

Dan: "Sam! You ok?"

"Yeah……………………..I'm ok…………………….kinda.

I've just blown up the engine in my brand spanking new Porsche that jerk at the factory said I don't deserve."

Turned out the car was just fine. Belatedly I found out what Herr Kraut should have explained to me before leaving the factory: the Ferdinand Porsche designed four-cylinder engine had to be reconfigured to meet more stringent 1968 US emission standards. A centrifugal pump was attached to the exhaust system to recirculate unburned fuel back through the engine. At high engine rpms the pump could turn as high as 13,000 rpms; when the engine rpms fell to idle the exhaust system would backfire.

An Iraqi IED could not have been louder.

Knowing how the engine would backfire came in handy on several occasions, but none more so than when I returned home to Bismarck in July, 1968, with Maryvonne, my French fiancée, in my 912.

Mom and Dad lived some ten miles from downtown, and traveled to and fro on River Road: two lanes, 45 MPH speed limit, that followed the base of the bluffs to the east of the Missouri River.

One evening, as we were walking out the front door to take in a movie in downtown, Mom warned me about Deputy Sheriff Bennie:

"He looks just like Barney Fife on 'Andy of Mayberry.' He's scared to death of me because I chewed him out when he drove too fast on the dirt road when Sean (my much younger Down Syndrome brother) was playing in the yard (probably wearing only his diaper, which is all we could keep on him). But I just know he wants to get back at me by citing one of you kids for any traffic violation."

"Yeah, yeah," I thought.

I had the Porsche in fifth gear, going about ninety miles per hour, when we topped a hill, only to run into Deputy Bennie in his prowler.

His eyes grew as large as saucers when he saw me. He turned on the gumball machine light on top of his car. I immediately braked and pulled over to the shoulder. I had the tach topped at 5,000 RPM as I switched off the ignition.

I said to Maryvonne, "Watch this."

I had pulled over near the top of the hill. To our right was a steep embankment that sloped to a small stream.

In the rear-view mirror I watched Deputy Bennie get out of his car and saunter towards mine. I saw a smirk on his face. He just knew he had me dead to rights. I rolled down the window.

"Going a little fast, weren't you?"

"Maybe. Wasn't paying attention."

"Just how fast, do you think?"

"Seventy or so."

"The speed limit is forty-five. Let me see your license."

I pushed it through the open window to him.

"You Vi McQuade's kid?!"

"Yes I am."

Handing back my license, ""Well slow this bomb down!"

When he got even with my tail pipe I hit the ignition switch.

KABOOM!!!!

The last I saw of Deputy Bennie in the rear-view mirror, the soles of his shoes were rotating as he rolled down the embankment into the stream.

When we returned home after the movie, I told Mom about the encounter with Deputy Bennie. Laughing, she said in her inimitable farm girl, Rosey Riveter way, "Serves that dumb son-of-a-bitch right!"

As I wrote earlier, in ten months I drove my Porsche 912 about 20,000, mostly in France, but also other European countries. I shipped it to the States from France in June, 1968. In October I sold it to a guy in Minneapolis for the same factory price I had paid.

It was a long, sad bus ride from Minneapolis back to the campus of St. John's University, where I was completing my senior year.

Forty-six years passed before, in 2014, I purchased my second Porsche: a used metallic silver 2012 911 Carrera S Cabriolet.

I cannot explain why I waited so long. In those intervening years I owned three Mercedes sedans, one a 300E AMG, and a 2003 50 year anniversary Z06 Corvette. Before buying the Vette I tried to make a deal on a used 911 S 4WD with a salesman at a Porsche dealership in Minneapolis, but he never got back to me, a surreal experience I have had on several attempts at buying cars. When I mentioned my desire to buy another Porsche to the head of the service department of the GMC dealership where I bought my pickups, he said, "This is what you will have to do *WHEN* it breaks down: lift it on a flat-bed truck, return it to Minneapolis, fly there when it is repaired, and be prepared to pay at least $2,000. Is that what you want in life?"

But he must have been thinking of the 911 models T, L, and S that I could not afford nor justify when I bought my '68 912; they did have a bad reputation for being temperamental, something about the valves needing constant adjustment. I am now on my third and fourth Porsches; so far they have been indestructible.

The summer of 2015 I drove the Carrera S from Bismarck, ND, to the East Coast, taking one month, covering more than 5,000 miles. I very much enjoyed the drive, except for the potholes, mostly in upstate New York and New York City; I was lucky to see several of them in time to swerve, or I would have lost a wheel or part of the undercarriage.

En route my friends all wanted a ride with the top down, which I never much cared for nor did much myself. Whenever I did I felt like I was in a fishbowl. Especially at stoplights. I couldn't pick my nose without people in the other cars pointing at me and laughing.

That Porsche 911 S Carrera was the best car I had owned to date, including the Z06 Corvette; I just felt more comfortable in it. But ever since I could not afford to buy any of the 911 T, L, and S models when I bought my 912 at the factory, I had always wanted to own a top-of-the-line Porsche.

So that September I drove to the Porsche dealership in Fargo, ND, to discuss ordering a 911 Turbo for delivery the following spring; I was thinking Black with a natural leather interior.

While I was there a new white 911 Turbo was being unloaded from the transport truck. I thought I would just check out the interior: two tone natural leather. The car also had all the extras I probably would have ordered myself, including 18 way seats and Burmeister Sound System.

I liked the car. And the white color was growing on me, making more and more sense; I had a big, black SUV that was a pain to keep clean.

I also had this thought: "Sam, you are 67 years old, burning, now, some serious daylight. Do you really want to wait for your dream Porsche for spring delivery?"

I bought it on the spot for pick up the following week.

I never told my wife.

When I returned to Bismarck with the 911 Turbo, parking it in our house garage, I said, "I have something to show you."

She has never been impressed by cars. When I met her in France in 1967, she was driving a '50s Citroen Deux Chevaux: 2 cylinder, 18 hp engine car with a canvas top, a tin can of a car with bug-eyed headlights. But it got 50 miles per gallon, which was important even in that era when gas was far more expensive than in the States.

Her reaction when she saw my new baby?

"I like the color better."

The following summer, 2016, I drove the Turbo through the South and the Deep South over a six week, 7,150 mile drive through twenty-five states.

I got a lot of looks.

In a gas station/convenience store in Texarkana, Arkansas, while I was fueling, at least six people came out of the store to take pictures of my car. One cracker-looking dude remarked, "Golly! Lookee here! We ain't never seen no vee-hi-cuuule, the likes of which y'all got here!"

I had just driven 179 miles on a two-lane road in the Ozark Mountains. It was straight out of "The Beverly Hillbillies." I had never seen so much road kill in my life: skunks, possums, which I expected, but also armadillos, which I had thought only existed in Texas. Ol' Granny Clampett would have henpecked me for not picking up the possum and armadillo carcasses for her to cook, a practice, I learned, that is common in those parts.

I had also never seen so many Baptist churches, most right next to each other in the small towns through which the road ran, every one of which also had its County Mountie parked at the town entrance to catch and fine speeding drivers. I had been forewarned; I slowed from 100 mph to the local speed limit as soon as I saw the sign: "Welcome to Hicksville."

The Baptist pastors all seemed to be trying to outdo one another with their witty signs alongside the road to attract fresh souls. The best:

"God loves religious fruit. He doesn't love religious nuts."

Porsche Driving Schools

Through my Porsche dealer in Fargo, North Dakota, I learned about the Porsche Driving School in Birmingham, Alabama. He said, "Sam, you are now driving race cars. You need to learn how to drive them the way they were meant to be driven."

He was right.

Now, after four Porsche driving schools, while I would never compare myself to the likes of any professional racer, I am a much more capable – and alert -- driver.

Porsche Performance Driving Course, Barber Motorsports Complex, Birmingham, Al, December, 2014

The majority of Porsche USA's Driving Schools are conducted on the grounds of the Barber Motorsport Complex near Birmingham, Alabama, which includes a museum housing the world's largest collection of motorcycles, a 2.4 mile road circuit, grandstands for an annual Indy Car race, and numerous concrete parking lots that are used to teach students a variety of driving techniques.

The two-day course began with a one hour class. Following introductions of the instructors and class participants, the lead instructor asked, "What wins races on road circuits?"

We answered in unison. "Speed."

"Nope. It's braking."

This seemed counterintuitive.

"What?"

On the screen at the front of the classroom appeared the outline of a Porsche 911 about to enter a ninety degree hairpin turn.

"What will happen if this car carries too much speed into this turn? It will never make it to the exit point, right? It will slide off the track and crash if there is a barrier. So how should the driver negotiate this?"

He went on to explain the braking point before entry, trail (tapering) braking to just before the apex of the turn, but allowing the car to carry momentum around the apex, then squeezing on the accelerator at the exit point to gain speed on the following straightaway.

He then put up a slide showing the outline of the road circuit at the Barber Complex: sixteen turns of varying radii, including one ninety degree hairpin, a "corkscrew," and a section of "esses;" only four short straightaways.

"The fastest way around this track involves more braking and braking technique than stepping on the gas."

Sounded simple enough.

Just try it on a racetrack when your competitive instincts are screaming at you for speed, and more speed, especially when a competitor's car shows up behind yours for a pass.

It wasn't until the last track session on the third and final day of my fourth Porsche Driving School (Masters Plus) that I felt I had driven the Barber road circuit the way it was meant to be driven. It was a proud moment, made even prouder when the six instructors who were stationed at various points to observe and grade our driving, concurred.

I didn't let it go to my head.

Although I had passed several cars, I got passed by another driver. My consoling thought: "I am sixty-nine years old, and probably shouldn't even be doing this. He's much younger and doesn't yet have my fear of mortality."

The instructor also showed us a series of slides depicting how tire traction changes during braking, accelerating, and in turns, due to weight shift. Braking causes the car's nose to dip, increasing traction on the front tires, decreasing traction in the rears; accelerating causes the reverse. He said the goal in racing is to minimize abrupt changes. "Smoother is better, whether braking, accelerating, or moving the steering wheel."

The Porsche Performance Course consists of two days about evenly divided between a variety of driving exercises and track time. Track time is about fifty per cent "follow the leader" behind one of the instructors so students get hands-on knowledge of braking points and other nuances, and fifty per cent driving solo, when students get to drive as fast as they desire, as long as they are safe. Passing is not allowed.

Our class, numbering about thirty participants, was divided into smaller groups. For my group's first exercise we were driven to a concrete parking lot on which were arranged orange florescent cones in roughly a figure eight pattern. A mid-engine Porsche Cayman was parked at the start/finish line.

Instructor: "This is the autocross track. The goal is to lap the course in the least amount of time without knocking over cones, for which there is a penalty of five seconds for each cone. To do that you will need to learn two things: where and how much to brake; and to turn your head to see the exit point of the hairpin turns. Your hands will steer the car where your eyes are looking. So always look ahead."

I was given this same advice when I was learning to ride single track trails on my mountain bike: "Look ahead." Looking down at the front tire is a recipe for an "End-O," that is, flipping bodily over the handlebars, which can be hard on one's back, not to mention one's ego.

We took turns driving the Cayman with the instructor in the passenger seat barking instructions: "Brake here! Brake harder! Speed up! Too fast! Just knocked over a cone!"

And always the same question: "Where are you looking?"

None of us started out well.

It was frustrating.

But after a few initial laps we began to get the hang of it, making faster, more controlled laps.

And looking ahead.

For the second exercise we walked to another lot with a sloped concrete surface covered in black epoxy; on the higher edge jets sprayed a constant wave of water; florescent orange cones were arranged in two half circles. The instructor motioned for us to gather round him as he stood next to a Porsche 911 Carrera S.

"This is the Skid Pad. The idea here is to drive the car on this slick surface around the half-circles of cones in a figure eight pattern. The right speed combined with the right amount of braking, the car will not skid. Too much speed into the turns combined with too much braking will make the car understeer. Have you heard the racing term, 'tight?' That is understeer; the car doesn't turn in the direction of the steering wheel, but plows ahead. Stepping on the gas too early and too hard will make the car oversteer. In racing it is called 'loose;' the rear of the car shoots out and away from the line, causing the car to spin. Or do a 'cookie,' as we like to call it.

Who wants to be the first victim?"

We all managed to understeer and, especially, oversteer the car, several guys even doing a couple of "cookies" in a row.

But I made fewer mistakes than the others in my group. At the end of my session, the instructor asked me, "Where did you learn to drive this well on slick surfaces?"

"In Bismarck, North Dakota, when I had my driver's license at age fourteen, in Mom's massive 1948 Buick Roadmaster sedan. I practiced doing 'shit hooks,' now, in our age of PC, more politely termed 'cookies,' on snow and ice-covered streets without hitting parked cars. Driving a Porsche on this is a piece of cake in comparison."

The Barber Motorsports Complex is Porsche heaven.

By my estimate the inventory of nearly all the models Porsche makes has to exceed ten million dollars in value. At this introductory course we drove Boxters, Caymens, Panamera sedans, Cayenne SUVs, and 911 Carreras with both manual and PDK automatic transmissions.

I was told that the full-time staff of instructors, all former race drivers, numbers fifty plus. Not to mention the staff of mechanics whose mission is to maintain the cars in racing condition.

To my knowledge Porsche is the only automobile manufacturer with such a costly commitment to performance driving; it has driving schools in the US, South America, China, and a number of European countries.

I learned that the Porsche models at Barber are rotated out after one year or ten thousand miles, whichever comes first. They are completely gone over, repaired and repainted as necessary, recertified to Porsche standards, and sold at dealer auction. I asked the young man who is head of maintenance if he would ever be willing to buy a Porsche that had been driven by neophyte schmucks like us. He said, "Absolutely! These are the best maintained Porsches in the US."

Porsche Driving Schools are not cheap. But I don't think most participants know or appreciate the extent of the costs involved. I was shocked when one instructor told my group during a lunch break that the soft compound rubber tires on the cars last on average only three hundred miles. He said, "Michelin and Pirelli provide them to us free of charge. Without their participation you fellows would never pay the price we would have to charge."

When I asked him why Porsche makes such an investment, he replied, "To sell cars. Sam, you wouldn't believe how many students return home with the intent to purchase a Porsche model they drove here or to upgrade to a faster model."

Happened to me.

One afternoon my group got to drive Porsche Cayenne SUVs on primitive steep roads in the wooded hills adjacent to the Barber Complex. In one section I had my Cayenne balancing on just two wheels, the other two hanging in the air. I have owned many makes and models of off-road, four-wheel drive vehicles in my life. But nothing like that!

When I returned home I called the dealer in Fargo about his Cayennes in inventory; I bought a Black Cayenne Turbo, an SUV with a top-end of 173 mph!

When he delivered it to Bismarck, I noticed a sticker on the left side of the dashboard with 150 over 240 printed on it. I asked him what it meant.

"Porsche doesn't want you to drive this Cayenne faster than 150 MPH (240 kilometers per hour)."

"But it is capable of going faster than that."

"True. But it is equipped with all-terrain tires. You would run the risk of shredding them."

"Oh don't worry about it."

The various driving exercises during the Performance Course are a wonderful introduction to the capabilities of a number of different Porsche models.

But none more so than "Launch Control."

After lunch the second day my group was told we would be driven to "Launch Control."

We asked, "What's that?"

"You'll find out!"

On a concrete parking lot was a red 911 Turbo S pointing down a lane between two rows of florescent cones. Our instructor told us that we would get to drive it three times.

When my turn came I got seated and buckled the safety belt.

The instructor explained: "Step on the brake with your left foot; slam on the accelerator with your right; the tachometer needle will jump to red-line, but it won't hurt the engine, as it is computer controlled; when a yellow light with "Launch Control" appears on the dashboard, let go of the brake. But! And this is important. First make sure your helmet is firmly pushed back into the top of the seat. This is like a catapult launch off an aircraft carrier; it won't snap your neck, but it could make it pretty sore."

Stepping on the brake, I pushed my helmet back, and floored the accelerator. The engine screamed like it was about to tear from the chassis, and I could feel the car wanting to surge forward. The yellow "Launch Control" light appeared. I released the brake.

It felt like god had just drop-kicked me in the behind.

The two rows of cones became blurs. I had to jump on the brake to avoid going off the end of the lot.

I had just experienced zero to sixty miles per hour in under three seconds.

That 911 Turbo S had 560 horsepower with computer-controlled all-wheel drive to adjust torque to each wheel as needed. There had been no tire squeak at the start.

Only the sensation of pure acceleration.

In the bar that night a fellow student asked what I thought was the best part of the Performance Driving Course, and I said, "Hands down! Launch Control."

He told me he loved to drive his 911 Turbo S to the drag strip in Houston.

"Kids show up with their souped-up cars and pour Hilex on the tires for the burnout.

Me? I just sit at the start line with the engine idling and the air-conditioning on.

It's never even close.

When the race is over it is really fun to see the look of shock on their faces. They can't believe my little car just beat hell out of theirs."

At the end of the second day we all got to ride "shotgun" with one of the instructors on a "hot lap." After all the talk emphasizing driving smoothness, and sometimes being criticized when I wasn't, I was more than surprised at how my instructor drove the car. Half the time he had it nearly sideways, rapidly jerking the steering wheel to avoid flying off the track. At the end he asked me what I thought of his "hot lap."

I said, "To be honest I am confused. You just drove exactly the opposite way we were told, and the way I have been trying to drive these past two days."

He just shrugged his shoulders. "That's racing."

I didn't say anything. But it made me wonder how many races he had won in his career.

Porsche One-on-One Coaching, Circuit Bugatti, Le Mans, France, April, 2015

This was one of a variety of one-day courses offered by the Porsche Driving Center located near the grandstands and control tower of the 24 Hours of Le Mans race.

I had this preconceived idea that I would be driving on at least part of the Circuit de la Sarthe, the road track for the 24 Hours. That would have been really cool!

But no.

Just like the Performance Driving Course in Birmingham, this course began with a classroom session. The lead instructor asked us in French to introduce ourselves, state which make and model car we drove, and whether we had any prior performance driving training. The group numbered about twenty; most of us drove Porsches; only a few had prior training. I discovered that I was the only foreigner; all the other participants were French.

Not that we would be racing, but I expected to see better driving skills from this group than the one in Birmingham. Because the average French driver drives much better and far more aggressively, but more safely than the average American driver. There are good reasons why this is so. Driver's Education is mandatory in France. The written, oral, and actual driver's exams to qualify for a license are far more stringent and exacting. Plus secondary roads in France, with their narrow driving lanes and twists and turns, resemble road racing circuits, but with traffic.

The instructor continued with a similar explanation to the one we got in Birmingham about driving techniques for negotiating turns: entry braking point, trail-braking to the apex, a bit of drift around the apex, and squeezing the accelerator at the exit point.

At the end of the class we were each paired with another participant and introduced to our driving coach, whom we would share throughout the day-long experience. This was a disappointment, as I had this preconception that I would have a full day of one-on-one coaching, not a half day. As it turned out I was glad for it, because by the end of my last track session I was a complete dishrag.

I was paired with a guy from Paris who had a Porsche but no training in performance driving.

Jean-Luc, our coach, *LOOKED* like a race driver: young, slim, good-looking, black hair to his shoulders, a shadow of a beard, strutting with that French "je m'en fiche" ("don't give a damn") confidence.

Our first track session took place on a road circuit about the same 2.4 mile length as the track at Barber. I thought I would impress my coach, since I had been at the Performance Course just four months prior. But my competitive nature took over; I drove too fast, forgetting most everything I had learned about race braking. When he yelled something in French at me, given the high-pitched engine whine and the thickness of my helmet, I had to yell back "Quoi?" each time. "What?" At one point I must have really messed up, because Jean-Luc reached over and slapped my hand.

Most embarrassing.

Later a barrier was taken down to lengthen the circuit to about 5.5 miles. Jean-Luc did a demonstration drive for each of us to familiarize us with the layout and show braking points. Later, when I was struggling with one section, he drove another, after which I did much better. At the end of the day he told me, "You got this."

I was rather proud of myself.

On one of my last laps I had glanced down at the end of the longest straightaway to see 235 kilometers per hour showing on the digital speedometer, 140 miles per hour.

Doesn't sound that fast?

Try it sometime.

Over a glass of champagne Jean-Luc asked me what my thoughts were on the day. I said, "It was a great experience, and I learned a lot from you about racing. But I am disappointed that there was no section on the track to drive 195 miles per hour."

He asked, "Why would you even think you would do that?"

"Well, the top-end speed of the Porsche 911 Carrera S is 195 MPH."

"So?"

"Where is the Mulsanne Straight? LMP1 prototypes have been known to go as fast as 250 MPH on it."

He then explained something I had never known before. Except for the start/finish straight in front of the main grandstands and the Esses at the iconic half-tire Dunlop Bridge, the 24 Hours of Le Mans endurance race is run on public roads.

Porsche Masters Course, Barber Motorsports Complex, Birmingham, AL, June, 2015

The two day Masters Course agenda is similar to the Performance Course: autocross, skid pad, trail braking, but with no "Launch Control" or off-road driving, allowing for more track time. The biggest difference is participants are allowed to pass slower vehicles on three of the four straightaways under strict rules: slower drivers need to watch for cars behind them, flash their signal lights, and pull to one side to allow the pass.

On my first demonstration laps I was fortunate to be paired with Chief Instructor Hurley Heywood, a three time champion driver at Le Mans, twice with Porsche. His driving was smoothness personified. His "hot lap" was nothing like I had experienced at the end of the Performance Course. He drove it as fast, if not faster, but without any of the tire screeching sideways movements, his hands barely moving the steering wheel.

Now I was really confused!

At lunch I commented on the difference to one of the main instructors.

"What's the name of the instructor you were with last time?"

"Sorry. I don't remember. He's not here at this course."

"Well, try to drive like Hurley, not that guy."

Porsche Masters Plus Course, Barber Motorsports Complex, Birmingham, AL, July, 2016

By the end of the Masters Course I felt I had become a better driver, but I wasn't satisfied that I had become a good driver, able to drive the racing line as it was designed; I continued to struggle in several of the sixteen turns.

I hoped what I would learn at the three day Masters Plus Course might change that. During the opening classroom session we were told that if the instructors deemed our driving to be worthy, we would be granted certificates to participate in SCCA and Porsche Club of America racing competitions. This became my personal goal. Not that at the age of sixty-nine I was going racing. It was a "bucket list" thing.

This "carrot" incentive came with a warning: three black flags for violating rules or driving in an unsafe manner would result in expulsion from the school.

I was fortunate to be paired once again with Hurley Heywood for my demo laps. I paid close attention, trying to memorize his movements and his explanations of proper braking points, when to trail brake, where to accelerate and coast, and his driving line. He told me something that stayed with me the next three days of the course: "To go faster use all of the track."

In addition to autocross, skid pad, and trail braking exercises, the twenty-four participants, divided into two groups, had four track sessions per day, two in the morning and two in the afternoon. Temperatures all three days were in the mid-nineties and the air was suffocating heavy with humidity. By the end of the second day my body felt as beat up from G forces as the hits I had taken in the first days of high school summer twice-per-day full-contact football practices.

I also had an open wound about the size of a fifty cent coin on the outside of my left knee; the skin had been rubbed down to raw flesh from the speaker cover of the Bose sound system in the driver side door. We began calling it the "cheese grater." One instructor laughed, "You now have the Porsche Red Badge of Courage. You need to wear pants, not shorts." In spite of the heat I followed his advice for the third day.

At the end of the course our entire class was granted racing certificates. In spite of a few black flags -- one guy got two, I had none -- the lead instructor said all the instructors agreed that we were the best class of participants in memory.

I was proud of what I had accomplished. As I wrote earlier, at the end of my final track session I felt like I had driven the circuit the way it was intended. Best, the six instructors who were stationed at various points to observe and grade our driving concurred.

For three years I had been invited to drive my Porsche 911 for a day on the circuit at Brainerd International Raceway, near Brainerd, Minnesota, the birthplace of the myth of Paul Bunyan and his Blue Ox, Babe. The first two years I had conflicting plans. I seriously considered the invitation in 2016, as the track day was scheduled to take place only a few days after the Porsche Masters Plus Course.

I asked the organizer, "How many other participants? Who are they? Has any of them had performance driving training?"

"We limit it to twenty drivers. A couple of guys have Porsche GT3s and know what they are doing. The others show up with a mish-mash of cars including a couple of Porsche Boxters. To my knowledge you are the only driver who has had any training."

I declined.

Especially after I learned that track insurance for one day would cost $1,300 with a $10,000 deductible, the face value of the policy being $40,000 short of the replacement cost of a new 911 Turbo. Moreover, after a day of racing, on my return drive to Bismarck, I would probably have had to stop at the dealership in Fargo for new tires and brake pads.

No thank you.

I would much prefer to return to a Porsche Driving School at Barber Motorsports in Birmingham. I know it would be more fun and I would learn more than at Brainerd.

Plus, I would get to beat up Porsche's vehicles.

SOME 24 HOURS OF LE MANS FACTS AND FIGURES

- First race: 1923
- Years race cancelled: 1936 (civil unrest); 1940-1948 (WWII)
- 2016: 84th running of the 24 Hours
- Course distance: changes constantly. Originally: 17.262 kilometers (10.7 miles). 2016: 13.629 kilometers (8.44 miles).
- Course layout: 21 turns; 9 left, 12 right; 50 gear changes per lap
- Average top speed (Hunadieres Straight): 340 KPH (210 MPH)
- Average speed slowest turn (Virage Arnage): 75 KPH (52 MPH)
- Distance covered in 1923: 2,209 kilometers (1,369 miles); average speed: 92 KPH (57 MPH)
- Distance covered (average) in modern era: 5,300 kilometers (3,286 miles); average speed: 240 KPH (148 MPH)
- Most distance all-time: 5,422 kilometers (3,362 miles), 2010, Audi R15

- Most laps all-time: 389, 2010, Audi R15
- Fastest speed all-time: 405 KPH (252 MPH) in 1988 by Roger Dorchy in a Welter Racing "Project 400" car
- Fastest lap in race: 3 minutes 17 seconds in 2015 by Andre Lotterer in an Audi R18 e-tron Quattro
- Most races participated: 33, Henri Pescarolo (France) between 1966 and 2009
- Most victories: Tom Kristensen (Denmark) between 1997 and 2013
- Most successful Marques: Porsche with 18 victories; Audi 13, Ferrari 9
- 24 winning Marques: Alfa Romeo, Aston Martin, Audi, Bentley, BMW, Chenard & Walker, Delahaye, Ferrari, Ford, Jaguar, Lagonda, La Lorraine, Matra, Mazda, McLaren, Mercedes, Mirage, Peugeot, Porsche, Renault
- Most cars all-time: 60
- Highest per cent cars finishing: 90.9%, 30 of 33 in 1923
- Lowest per cent cars finishing: 13.7 %, 7 of 51 in 1970
- Most 1-2 finishes: Porsche: 12

- Most second place finishes without winning: Toyota: 5
- Most consecutive pole positions: Porsche: 6
- Smallest winning margin: 20 meters, 1966 between two Ford GT40s
- Largest winning margin: 349 kilometers (216 miles), 1927, Bentley
- Number of drivers killed: 24

THE 24 HOURS OF LE MANS

This is not intended as a history of the 24 Hours of Le Mans Endurance Race, only *SOME* history, and some things I find interesting.

Many histories of the race have been written. I purchased one in a store at the racetrack that could be the most in-depth: "Les 24 Heures du Mans Pour Les Nuls," "The 24 Hours of Le Mans For Idiots." After 416 pages of year-by-year chapters detailing the cars, the drivers, changes in the racetrack, even societal conditions that affected given races, I had most of my questions answered. But I have not found it in an English translation. Sorry.

The 24 Hours of Le Mans is the most prestigious race in the world.

The Indianapolis 500 bills itself as "The Greatest Spectacle in Racing." Maybe it is. As spectacle. Typically it is run in under three hours. The track is 2.5 miles around, so fans in the grandstands can view the majority of the race. Same with NASCAR races.

Compare them to Le Mans: 24 unrelenting hours, the winning car traveling over six times more distance than at Indy or NASCAR and eighteen times more than a Grand Prix.

During the 2016 Le Mans race I asked a retired endurance race driver how an Indy Car or a NASCAR might perform in the 24 Hours. He said the Indy car's lap speeds would be close to those of the LMP1 hybrid prototypes, but wouldn't last. As to NASCAR: "It's been tried. The cars failed miserably. A modern NASCAR would be turning laps thirty to forty seconds slower than the prototypes. Eventually something on them would blow. Endurance racing requires durability in both man and machine."

Regarding the man "...in both man and machine," in the early days a couple of drivers attempted to run solo, but this was banned as too dangerous. Until the 80s the rule was a minimum of two drivers. As racing technology evolved, making for faster cars, especially in the turns, producing higher G-forces, the rule was changed to a minimum of three drivers. And no driver is allowed to race more than four hours in a six hour stretch and no more than fourteen hours in total.

How do three drivers manage to maintain their sharpness over the 24 Hours of Le Mans? Another former driver told me that learning to rest and relax and unwind is extremely important. "The body can be conditioned to do this. During a couple of races I even slept a bit between stints behind the wheel. A driver must have full concentration. This place is dangerous under ideal conditions. It is more dangerous when it rains and at night. It is at its most dangerous in the rain at night."

Another former driver told me, "The race can be lost on the first lap. It can be lost on the last lap. Le Mans is the ultimate test of sustained concentration coupled with patience."

In the early years the cars that ran the 24 Hours of Le Mans were sport models of makes manufactured for the motoring public. Eventually factory prototypes were allowed. There are now two categories: LMP (Le Mans Prototype) and GT (Gran Touring; models that the public can purchase). These categories are divided in two classes: LMP1, the fastest, with enclosed cockpit; LMP2, different weight, power output, open cockpit allowed; GT Endurance Pro, factory entries, and GT Endurance AM, privately funded teams.

Safety

Racing is inherently dangerous. At any moment anything can go wrong with either car or driver.

Or both.

The famous Formula One champion, Jackie Stewart, on racing in the 60s and early 70s: "In those days racing was dangerous, sex was safe."

Today it is rare for a driver to be seriously injured, and much rarer to be killed.

During the 2016 race the Pit Boss of Greaves Motorsports explained to me how modern racecars are designed and manufactured for maximum driver safety. Chassis and body shear points are computer designed around a cockpit cocoon, then crash-tested. "If it is determined that the new design does not protect the driver, it's back to the drawing board."

Spectator safety has also become paramount. Race fans go to tracks to watch a race, not to be injured or killed.

For too many years none of this was so.

Even a cursory review of the early, and not-so-early, history of automobile racing reveals a near criminal disregard of safety for either drivers or spectators.

Look at the old pictures, the old film footage, the movies about racing: open cockpit racecars without so much as a seat belt, not to mention a roll bar, that in an accident transformed into exploding balls of fire and shrapnel. And spectators were allowed to watch while standing unprotected adjacent to the track. If barriers existed at all they were at best minimal: neck high wood fascines at the base of the grandstands.

Over the years a number of races, mostly on road circuits, were declared too dangerous and summarily halted or the courses altered dramatically; the Targa Florio in Sicily and Monza in Italy are examples.

While more drivers have been killed at Daytona, Monza, Indianapolis, and the Nuburgring Nordschleife than at Le Mans, its history is dark.

With the darkest moment in the history of racing: Saturday, June 11, 1955.

It was 6:28 pm, the race in its first hours. Near the right end of one of the start/finish grandstands a factory team Mercedes, driven by Frenchman Pierre Levegh, went airborne after hitting the left rear of a Jaguar that had swerved to avoid a collision. The car hurtled the fascine barrier and smashed into the crowd, exploding on impact in a black cloud of shrapnel. The force of the impact tore the motor from its mounts, rocketing it at head-level across the crowd.

To this day there are conflicting figures for the number of spectators killed and injured, but 82 and 120, are the most often cited.

The Mercedes factory team withdrew its other cars out of respect, never to return to Le Mans.

Unbelievably the race was allowed to continue. Race officials decided correctly that a panicked crowd of some two hundred thousand would clog the roads around the city of Le Mans, thus blocking ambulances arriving from surrounding towns.

The effects of this catastrophe were cataclysmic in the world of automobile racing. All racing, but particularly the 24 Hours of Le Mans, was called into question. At the very least something had to be done to increase spectator safety. At Le Mans the track entrance to the grandstands was curved to slow the cars, the stands were recessed and their bases raised up above the track, and high steel posts and fences installed. As time proved, the changes didn't provide complete safety. But it was the beginning of many years of changes and tweaks to ensure that on-track accidents would not injure or, especially, kill spectators.

Driver safety evolved more slowly.

During his career in the 60s and early 70s, as a three-time World Champion Formula One driver, Jackie Stewart campaigned for improved driver safety.

After he retired, when asked if it was fair to say some people in that era just saw fatalities as part of the sport, he replied:

"Almost certainly. There was never any anger when somebody died, just sadness. There was no solution, only acceptance. And nobody worked it out; nobody said, 'How do we stop it?' The governing body wasn't doing it, the track owners weren't doing anything because it was going to cost money, and the team owners didn't want to do anything that would threaten an event because they wouldn't get their start money. We were killing between four and eight drivers a year. If you raced for five full seasons, there was a two-in-three chance that you were going to die. It was ridiculous."

The traditional start at Le Mans had the drivers standing on the opposite side of the track, facing the cars, lined up by engine displacement, and parked diagonally. When the French tricolor flag was dropped the drivers would sprint to their cars in a mad dash to jump in, get them started, and pull out to begin racing. It was a chaotic spectacle that often produced the first crashes of the race.

The drivers didn't have to bother with seat belts; there were none. Sometime in the sixties when seat belts were first installed, drivers wouldn't take the time to buckle-up, racing for up to three hours before exiting the car for the relief driver, who had the time during the pit stop to properly strap himself. This practice resulted in several deaths in the early hours.

In 1963 qualifying began, so the cars were lined up for the start by the lap times achieved.

In 1969, Belgian Jackie Ickx, driving for the Ford factory GT40 team, walked to his car by way of protest of the mad dash tradition, and properly buckled-up.

He won the race.

In 1970 the cars were lined up for the start with the drivers seated and properly strapped.

From 1971 and beyond the race has begun with a much safer rolling start.

Some Fun History

Some have called the Ford versus Ferrari battles in the 60s the "Golden Age of Le Mans."

It began in 1963, when the top suits at Ford learned Enzo Ferrari was putting his business up for sale, price: eighteen million dollars, pocket change for Henry Ford II, the grandson of the founder, Henry Ford. Henry II, like his grandfather, was one of the most powerful industrialists of his time.

After conducting due diligence on Ferrari's company, Ford submitted a contract to the famously irascible "consigliere" that was none to his liking, and he refused to sign. There is some evidence he never had any intention to sell his business to an American company. But the business needed a cash infusion; eventually he partnered with Fiat.

When the news was delivered to Henry II, who was himself no slouch in the irascibility department, and never one to be rebuffed, he declared Ford would commit all its resources to beat Ferrari where it mattered most: on the race track, but especially at Le Mans, the plum of international racing.

The following year, 1964, a micro second in terms of developing and testing a prototype racecar capable of winning the most brutal race in the world, Ford had three factory entries. None finished. Only a Ford powered Shelby Cobra Daytona finished in fourth place. Ferrari finished 1-2-3-5-6.

Henry II was not pleased.

In 1965, Ford had eleven entries in various configurations (GT40 Mark I, GT40 Mark II, and Shelby Cobra Daytona). Phil Hill, driving one of the new Mark IIs, was the surprising pole winner, having set a new lap record. But the only Ford to finish was a Shelby Cobra Daytona in eighth place. Ferrari finished 1-2-3.

It was a major embarrassment for everyone associated with Ford from the top execs down to the dealers.

The department heads at Ford Racing received a card with these encouraging words:

"You'd better win," Henry Ford II.

In 1966, Ford finished 1-2-3. Ford four-peated in '67, '68, and '69.

Traditionally the winning drivers drank a glass of champagne on the podium. In '67, Dan Gurney shook the bottle and sprayed Henry Ford II and his second wife, a much younger, hot Italian. That has been the tradition since.

Most Americans know about the Indianapolis 500 and NASCAR. Far fewer know about the 24 Hours of Le Mans. If they do, and they are Baby Boomers, they probably learned about it because of two popular Hollywood actors, Paul Newman and Steve McQueen. Newman finished second overall in 1979 in a Porsche 935. McQueen wanted to drive a Porsche 917 with Jackie Stewart in 1970, while also directing the film, "Le Mans," but he was prohibited from doing so by the producer because of insurance issues.

"Le Mans" is more documentary than the typical Hollywood film about racing. The race was filmed using cars specially outfitted with onboard cameras. The script was written after filming. But a documentary-like movie was more to McQueen's liking. He hated the racing film, "Grand Prix," starring James Garner, so much that he routinely urinated into Garner's flowerbed from his apartment balcony above Garner's.

SOME TECHNICAL STUFF

During the race I asked the Greaves Motorsports Pit Boss why they had an LMP2 category car and not a faster LMP1. He said, "Money. Typically only factory teams such as Porsche, Audi, and Toyota race LMP1 category cars. And there are years when a given manufacturer doesn't participate at all. Porsche returned in 2014 after a long absence. The Porsche racing team budget for this year is two hundred million Euros. We cannot compete with that."

Why would a manufacturer spend such a sum on racing? Two reasons: it sells cars; it provides a laboratory for technological innovation that translates into ever-improved streetcars.

It has been said that without the Indianapolis 500 cars would not have rear view mirrors. While this is absurd, it is a fact that the first rear view mirror appeared on a car driven by Ray Harroun in the first Indy 500 in 1911. It allowed him to drive solo; he won the race.

The 24 Hours of Le Mans has been witness to many automotive innovations in aerodynamics, engines, drivetrains, and brakes. Mirroring the driving public's interest in increased efficiency and more stringent government regulation, recently hybrid technology has become the norm in the LMP1 category. The ultimate goal is to develop electric only powered racecars.

The Porsche 919 Hybrid prototype that won Le Mans in 2015 and 2016 was designed based on rules changes in 2014 for the LMP1 class. No longer would the power output be regulated but energy consumption expressed in magajoules (energy units). Translation: not the energy that is put on the wheels, but the energy that flows into the fuel tanks and batteries with a maximum of eight megajoules allowed per 13.629 kilometer lap. The goal is greater efficiency through less waste of energy.

The 919 Hybrid has a 2,000 cc, 500 HP V4 cylinder internal combustion engine that powers the rear axle; the front axle is powered by an electric system that produces 400 HP. To meet the eight megajoule energy limit it returns electricity to the Lithium-ion battery cells via two recovery systems: front brakes and exhaust gasses.

Fascinating.

But don't ask me how this works.

I was a words major in college, not a gear head.

EXPERIENCING THE 24 HOURS OF LE MANS

Sometime this past winter I was paging through one of the monthly issues of "Panorama" magazine produced by the Porsche Club of America when something in the advertisement by Fast Lane Travel caught my eye: "Total Le Mans Experience."

Fast Lane Travel has a long relationship with Porsche; mostly it offers high-end touring trips during which guests drive Porsche models of their choice in exotic locales, stay in chateaux hotels, and dine in gourmet restaurants. One had previously interested me: a ten-day Porsche driving experience in Provence in southeast France. When I showed it to my wife, who is much more frugal than I, she said, "Too expensive. Besides we have been to all those places."

"But not in a new Porsche!"

(In her French accent) "You weell want to drive. And riding in your Porsche makes me seeck."

So that was the end of that.

After posting my interest in Le Mans on Fast Lane Travel's website, I received a call from Sven, who asked me if there was anything in my background that had piqued my interest. When I told him about my year in France, buying a Porsche 912 at the factory in Stuttgart, and wanting to attend the '68 race that was postponed from June to September due to a nation-wide student and labor strike, he said, "Sam, this trip is for you. The only way to get closer to the 24 Hours than the experience we offer is to drive one of the cars."

He then described their VIP experience: hospitality area at the track, best grandstand seats, pit passes, a helicopter ride above the track during the race, meeting former winning drivers…what am I leaving out? Oh, yeah: luxury suites in chateaux hotels, as opposed to the alternatives: tent cities or campers. At my age I don't do camping. I did when I was young. No more. Now my idea of roughing it is watching black and white TV and drinking vodka martinis from plastic cups.

I said, "Sounds good to me. How much?"

Not sure why I even asked.

Several years ago, after my wife and I had signed up for a cultural tour of Russia, I asked my local travel agent to quote me prices in both coach and first class for a round trip from Bismarck to Moscow with a stopover in Paris. She emailed me itineraries and prices; the cost in first class had me choking. When I told her I couldn't justify the price difference she said, "Sam! If you don't fly first class, your children will!"

After a moment during which my mind raced through my personal financial balance sheet and estate plan, I said, "You're absolutely right!"

The Fast Lane Travel 24 Hours of Le Mans Experience was exactly how I wanted to fill one of my life's top bucket list items. At age 69 I was burning serious daylight. "What the hell," I thought, "Why not? It's now or never."

The itinerary for the Le Mans experience had a Monday arrival in Le Mans and a Monday departure for Paris. Tuesday was Le Mans museum day; Wednesday, Loire Valley winery visit and tasting; Thursday, "Saving Private Ryan" tour of the D-Day Landing beaches, museums, and the Coleville U.S. Cemetery.

I would have liked to visit the Le Mans racing museum. As to the Loire Valley winery, my wife's family had a wine business that specialized in Loire Valley wines. I am a student of war history, and had spent three days the prior year touring the D-Day landing zones, all the museums, and both American and German cemeteries (Interesting sidebar: grave markers at the U.S. cemetery, crosses and Stars of David, are all white; the German graves are marked with an iron cross in black stone).

Thursday afternoon I arrived at the Le Mans rail station, after having spent a week on my own on France's Atlantic coast, and was met by Robin Donovan, retired fourteen-time Le Mans driver, the owner of Dettaglio, a travel company that specializes in VIP race experiences in Europe. After getting settled in my room in Chateau du Maurier, the owners welcomed our group with a glass of champagne. We then were driven to the Greaves Motorsports hospitality tent behind the main grandstands of the racetrack for final qualifying runs.

The 24 Hours of Le Mans schedule:

Wednesday	Free Practice	4 Hours @ 16:00
	Qualifying	2 Hours @ 22:00
Thursday	Qualifying	2 Hours @ 19:00
	Qualifying	2 Hour @ 22:00
Friday	Parade of Drivers	
Saturday	Warm Up	45 min @ 09:00
	Race Start	@ 15:00
Sunday	Race Finish	@ 15:00

The two Porsche 919 Hybrids had qualified 1-2 on Wednesday. Thursday is "Bump Day," when drivers go all out to move up the start grid.

While enjoying a catered gourmet dinner prepared by a Danish chef and his staff, we watched qualifying begin on live television feeds from various points on the racetrack. Greaves had three TVs in its hospitality area: two for the live feeds; one showing updated car positions.

The weather the entire week I was on the French west coast had been miserable with rain, wind, and unseasonably cold temperatures. The forecast for the days of the 24 Hours of Le Mans was not encouraging: warmer, but with rain and thunderstorms and occasional sun.

Before the first qualifying session was complete we were hit with a thunderstorm and a rain deluge of biblical proportions. After several hours race officials cancelled qualifying for the night; the start grid on Saturday would be in the order determined by qualifying on Wednesday.

After a short night at our chateau we were chauffeured Friday morning to a hotel for petit dejeuner and van ride on part of the Circuit de La Sarthe with 1988 Le Mans winner Jan Lammers of the Netherlands, who explained the nuances of several turns and the two chicanes that were installed to slow cars on the Hunadieres and Mulsanne Straights, where cars formerly attained speeds as high as 250 MPH, which was determined to be too dangerous; now the prototypes *ONLY* get up to about 230 MPH.

He also drove us to the "Mulsanne Bump," a short rise in the roadbed that was shaved down following several accidents with Mercedes cars that took flight when air funneled under their chassis, launching them into the tops of the pine trees in the adjacent thick forest. The drivers survived; the treetops had cushioned the landing.

Our Le Mans VIP kit included pit lane passes for Friday and prior to the race start on Saturday, when the cars are pushed out to their qualifying positions on the starting grid. The sixty pits, located under the length of the main grandstand, have an exterior pad for fueling, tire changing, and servicing and an enclosed garage for race preparation and repairs.

I walked the full length of pit row, stopping at Greaves, Ferrari, Corvette, Porsche, and Ford, returning to Le Mans for the first time since its wins in '66-'69, where I saw William Clay Ford Jr., the great grandson of Henry Ford, and nephew of Henry Ford II. In partnership with Chip Ganassi Racing, Ford was competing in the GTE Pro Class with four new Ford GTs.

I was surprised to see that most of the cars were being rebuilt, some from the chassis up, after Wednesday's practice and qualifying round, and the abbreviated first round on Thursday. The need for fresh parts for the twenty-four hour ordeal made sense, but if any new part was defective or underperformed the teams would only have forty-five minutes the next morning for repairs or adjustments.

After lunch in the famous Auberge des Hunadieres, next to the Hunadieres Straight, with five-time Le Mans winner, Sir Derek Bell of Britain, we were driven to the VIP hospitality tent in the main square in Le Mans Centre for the "Grand Parade des Pilotes," watched by some 180,000 spectators.

What I found interesting were the many vintage vehicles in which the drivers rode, including a white '69 Cadillac convertible with the tall shark fins and red bullet tail lights. Best, though, was the first parade entry, men and women from the former French colony of Tahiti, dressed in traditional skimpy native garb, dancing to native drums. It was a scene straight out of a painting by Paul Gaugin, the French expressionist, who had lived in Tahiti for a time and was enraptured by the island's beautiful, but heavy-set women. The dance troupe's women far outweighed the men; I guessed the lead dancer weighed somewhere north of three hundred pounds. But was she graceful! Her hand movements and pirouettes were ballerina-like.

Saturday: Race Start

The weather that morning was pleasant with clouds and intermittent sunshine. But the forecast contained the threat of showers.

At 13:00, 1:00 PM, we were on the grid as the cars began to be pushed out of the pit garages and into their qualifying positions. I noticed that all the cars had slick dry pavement racing tires.

Race marshals herded everybody off the track, and we took our seats on the left side of the main grandstand, from where we had a view of the cars on the starting grid and the start/finish line.

Rain began sprinkling. Which set off a mad dash from the pits as crews frantically pushed carts of grooved rain tires and jacks to their cars for a tire change before the 15:00 (3:00 PM) start.

During the pre-race ceremonies rain intensity increased. Which didn't dampen the mostly French crowd's enthusiasm for a rousing singing of "La Marseillaise," the French national anthem since the Revolution in the late eighteenth century. One of our Dettaglio hosts said that an American guest in a prior year had told him that hearing the French spectators sing their national anthem was worth the entire trip.

Traditionally the Honorary Grand Marshal drops the French tricolor flag to begin the race on a rolling start after a warm-up lap. I didn't know the Grand Marshall was Brad Pit until I returned to our hospitality tent. But if he dropped the flag, I didn't see it, because by then rain was falling in slanted sheets. The race began behind the safety car, and continued that way for six full laps before the rain stopped and the sun came out, drying out the pavement. Still, in the first hours, a number of cars spun out after hitting puddles of standing water in the washboard warning tracks on the turns.

Our seats were in the first row. In spite of the roof over us we were getting soaked, so most of us headed back to the hospitality tent to watch the race on television, the best way to view the entirety of the Circuit de la Sarthe.

Our group of eleven was divided into smaller groups for the afternoon visit of the Greaves pit, a beehive of activity even when the car was on the track. There was little room to stand out of the way of the crew; the garage was crammed with large tool chests, hoses, computer monitors, and, especially tires. Greaves had on-hand an inventory of both slick and grooved tires for a minimum of nine complete tire changes; from their previous races at Le Mans they calculated tire changes every forty-four laps or six hundred kilometers (370 miles).

The tire storage area of the pit was unbearably hot. The Pit Boss, our host, explained that the stacks of tires, which were covered with thick rubber-coated canvas, are heated to ninety degrees Fahrenheit to prepare them for the speeds of Le Mans. Which answered my question of why, unlike Indy or NASCAR, I saw little or no zig-zagging behind the safety car when the race was under the yellow caution flag.

Late in the afternoon we walked in the tunnel under the track to a grassy area near the Le Mans airfield, where a veritable air force of helicopters lifted and landed, flying spectators on two circles above the race complex, which resembles a small city of 300,000 people, ambling around the grandstands, in the shopping area, the amusement park with its Ferris Wheel, and fields of tents and campers. It was truly spectacular. A diagram of the layout of the track does not do it justice compared to seeing it from the air. Most impressive were the two straights, pine forest on both sides, where the racecars were going faster than our helicopter.

At dusk we were driven to three spots in the forest, where we stood behind barriers to watch as the cars, barely fifty feet away, whizzed by at up to 230 MPH. At the first stop it was still light enough to recognize numbers on the cars. As darkness fell the only way to tell the cars apart was by the sounds of the engines; the LMP1s and LMP2s emitted an unmistakable high pitched whine; Ferrari, Porsche, Aston Martin and Ford GTs had a lower whine; the Corvettes growled and rumbled.

Sunday: Race Finish

I was in the hospitality tent mid-morning and watched on television when the #5 Toyota LMP1 passed the #2 Porsche. Over the course of the next hours the Toyota stretched its lead. I had travelled to Le Mans not only to see the 24 Hours in person for the first time, but to watch a consecutive win by Porsche. I am a Porsche guy.

It didn't look good.

You know how the race ended: with silence in the Toyota pit; jubilation in Porsche's.

There was also jubilation in Ford's, as three of its four cars finished, placing 1-3-4 in the GTE Pro Class (Ferrari was second). It seemed appropriate that William Clay Ford Jr, Henry II's nephew, got hosed with champagne on the podium.

END OF THE 2016 RUNNING OF THE 24 HOURS OF LE MANS

Our VIP Le Mans experience ended with a champagne reception and gourmet dinner in the other of our group's two chateaux hotels.

It was a bittersweet moment for me.

For fifty years, ever since I was a college sophomore in 1966, I had wanted to attend the 24 Hours of Le Mans. It had been at the top of my personal bucket list.

Now it was over.

As Mom used to say, "Chicken today, feathers and guts tomorrow."

Will I return?

Doubtful. Now it's kind of "been there, done that."

But I will journey again with Fast Lane Travel. I am already signed up for their "Adrenaline Adventure," next May in Germany.

Looking forward to winning their 150 MPH pin after driving on the one German autobahn that still has no posted speed limit.

But wondering if they have pins for higher speeds if I drive faster than that.

Printed in Poland
by Amazon Fulfillment
Poland Sp. z o.o., Wrocław